HOW TO BE YOUR CAT'S BEST FRIEND

HOW TO BE YOUR CAT'S BEST FRIEND

BY P.C.VEY

A PLUME BOOK

PLUME
Published by the Penguin Group
Penguin Books USA Inc., 375 Hudson Street, New York, New York 10014, U.S.A.
Penguin Books Ltd, 27 Wrights Lane, London W8 5TZ, England
Penguin Books Australia Ltd, Ringwood, Victoria, Australia
Penguin Books Canada Ltd, 10 Alcorn Avenue, Toronto, Ontario, Canada M4V 3B2
Penguin Books (N.Z.) Ltd, 182–190 Wairau Road, Auckland 10, New Zealand

Penguin Books Ltd, Registered Offices: Harmondsworth, Middlesex, England

First published by Plume/Meridian, an imprint of Dutton Signet,
a division of Penguin Books USA Inc.

First Printing, June, 1994
10 9 8 7 6 5 4 3 2 1

 REGISTERED TRADEMARK—MARCA REGISTRADA

LIBRARY OF CONGRESS CATALOGING-IN-PUBLICATION DATA
Vey, P. C. (Peter C.)
    How to be your cat's best friend / P. C. Vey.
        p.   cm.
    ISBN 0-452-27214-9
    1. Cats—Caricatures and cartoons.   2. American wit and humor,
Pictorial.   I. Title.
NC1429.V57A4   1994
741.5'973—dc20
                                        93–47921
                                            CIP

Printed in the United States of America

BOOKS ARE AVAILABLE AT QUANTITY DISCOUNTS WHEN USED TO PROMOTE PRODUCTS OR SERVICES. FOR INFORMATION
PLEASE WRITE TO PREMIUM MARKETING DIVISION, PENGUIN BOOKS USA INC., 375 HUDSON STREET, NEW YORK, NEW YORK 10014.

For Tina

SEND HIM TO COOKING SCHOOL.
ACCORDING TO THIS YOU'RE SUPPOSED TO LET THE CAT STIR IT.

SHARE MORE OF YOUR EXPERIENCES WITH HER, EVEN IF IT TAKES FOUR YEARS AND NINETY-THREE THOUSAND DOLLARS.

P.C.VEY

TAKE HIM FISHING.

BOB'S FISH MARKET

P.C.VEY

TAKE HIM FISHING FOR REAL.

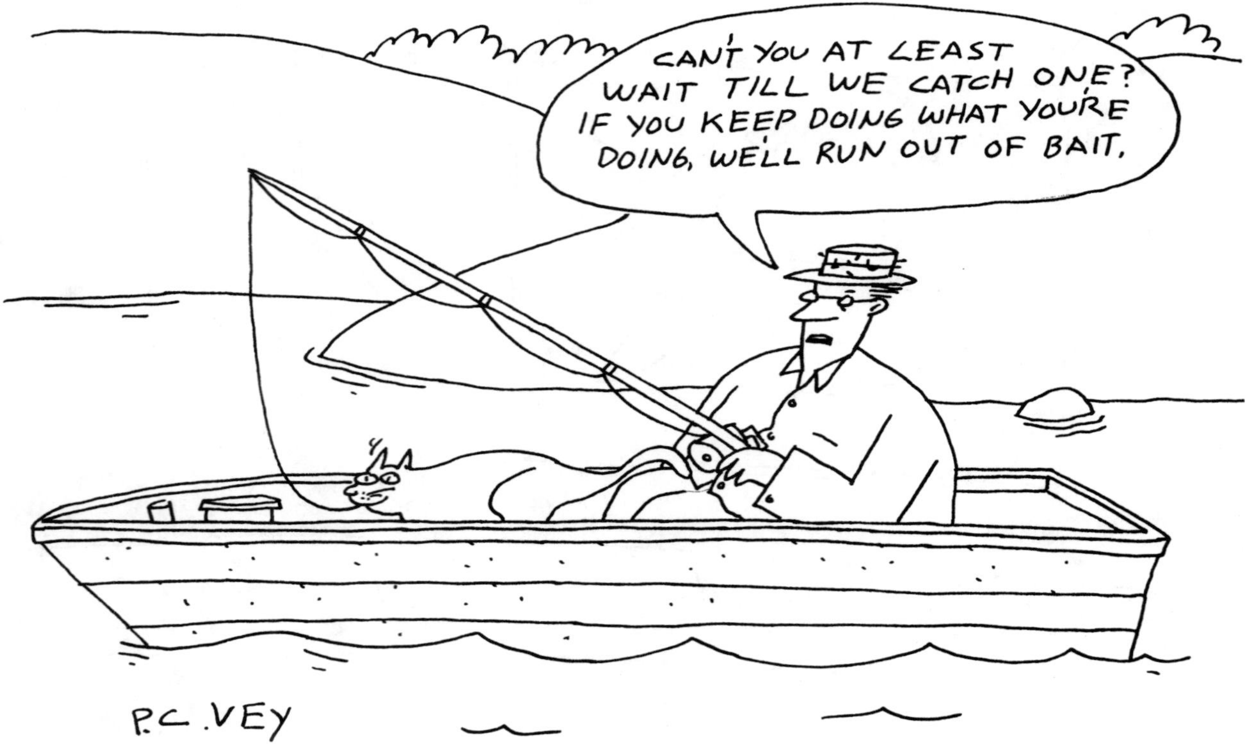

OPEN A STORE JUST FOR HIM.
CAN-O-FOOD
AT FIRST HE WAS GOING TO CALL IT "BOX-O-DRY FOOD"! BUT I SET HIM STRAIGHT.

BUY HIM AN AIRPLANE AND TEACH HIM TO FLY. CATS LOVE HEIGHTS. WHY DO YOU THINK THEY ALWAYS GET CAUGHT IN TREES?
WHO WANTS TO PET THE CAPTAIN? LAST CHANCE BEFORE WE LAND.

STICK UP FOR HIM EVEN THOUGH HE MIGHT BE IN THE WRONG.

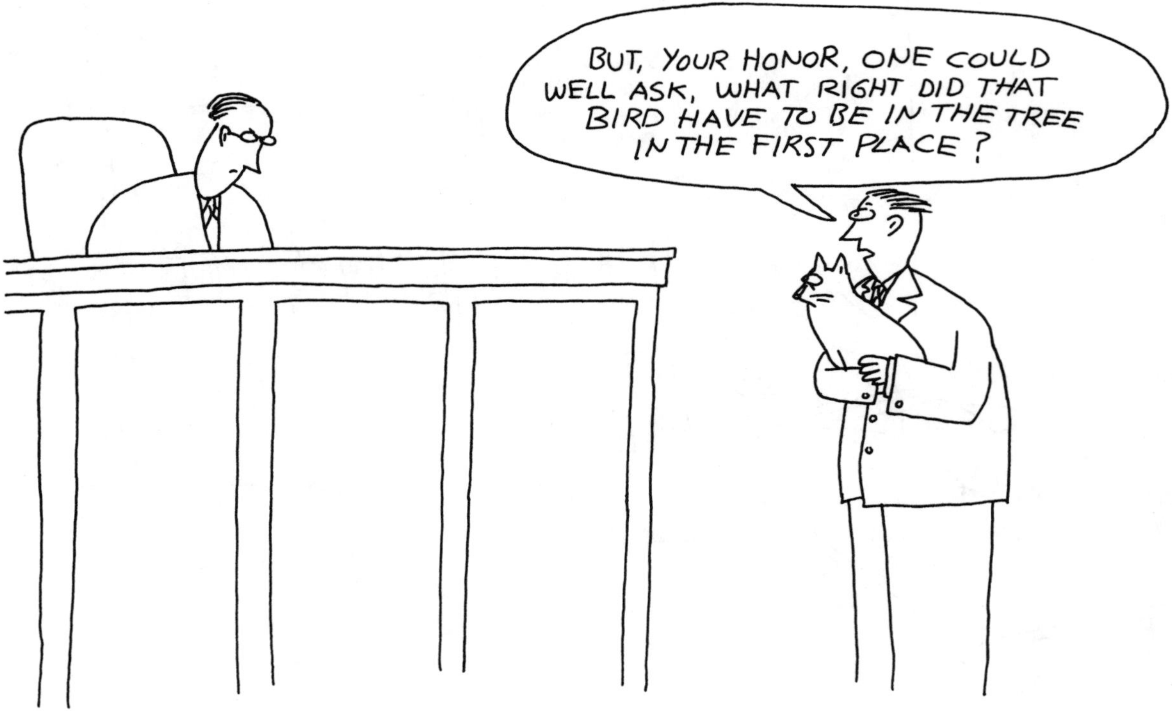

LET KITTY AND A FEW OF HER FRIENDS SIT IN ON YOUR NEXT BOARD MEETING.
OK THEN, SO IT'S THREE FOR, FOUR AGAINST, AND SEVEN MEOWS.